LOVE is...

Copyright © 2013 by S. D. Webb

All rights reserved under International and Pan-American Copyright Conventions.

Published and printed in the United States by Poetique Press, an imprint of Innovative Publishers, Inc., Boston, Massachusetts

Poetique Press is a trademark of Innovative Publishers, Inc.

Except as permitted under the United States Copyright Act of 1976, no part of this publication may be reproduced or distributed in any form or by any means, or stored in a data base or retrieval system, without the prior written permission of the publisher. For information contact Innovative Publishers Inc.

Published by
Innovative Publishers Inc.
PO Box 300446
Boston, MA 02130

Library of Congress Control Number: 2012950482

ISBN-13: 978-1884711138 Paperback
ISBN-10: 1-884711-13-8

ISBN-13: 978-1884711145 Hardback
ISBN-10: 1-884711-14-6

ISBN-13: 978-1884711183 Kindle
ISBN-10: 1-884711-18-9

ISBN-13: 978-1884711268 Audiobook
ISBN-10: 1884711-26-X

ISBN-13: 978-1884711329 iBook
ISBN-10: 1884711-32-4

10 9 8 7 6 5 4 3 2 1   13 14 15 16 17

Printed in the United States of America

First edition. February 2013

DEDICATION

I dedicate this poem book to my past and to my eager future.

CONTENTS

Acknowledgments		vii
Introduction		xi

1	I Don't Know Why	1
2	Just Because	3
3	Why?	5
4	Missing You (Part III)	7
5	Me and You	9
6	You're It (Me and You – Part II)	10
7	Denial (Part I)	13
8	Denial (Part II)	15
9	No Point	16
10	Some Thoughts	19
11	Hurting	21
12	No Luck	23
13	I'm Confused	25
14	Those Moments	27
15	Circles	29
16	Icon	31
17	Stupid Little Love Song	33
18	What is Love?	35
19	Words Form	37
20	Without Feeling	39
21	Broken	41
22	Hating This	43
23	Notice Me	45
24	Music is Love	47
25	Change	49
26	My New Life	51
27	No Explanation	53
28	Listen	54
29	Untitled	57
30	Pain Hurdles	59
31	Relapse	61
32	Open-ended Questions	63
33	Wrong Channel	65
34	Distance	67
35	Breakthrough	69

36	Light at the End	71
37	His Lips	73
38	I Found You	75
39	I am in love	77

ACKNOWLEDGMENTS

I would like to express my gratitude to the many people who saw me through my first book; to all those who provided support, talked things over, read, offered comments, and supported me at my first public reading.

"Give the lover an unlit candle and he will awaken it with his own Light".

—**Jalal'uddin Rumi**

INTRODUCTION

In a world where love is commonly perceived as an ancient cure for all things destructive, it is strangely ironic that most people are either unable to recognize love when it greets them, or only willing to accept certain aspects of the experience. Unfortunately, dismissing any facet of love, no matter how pleasant or unpleasant, is to interpret it as a one-dimensional reality, when it actually exists as an all-pervading phenomenon that reconstructs preexisting reality to define itself. After embarking on a journey to find this elusive phantom we call "love", it is not long before one realizes that the quest is similar to finding one's purpose in life, and perhaps rightly so since, consciously or unconsciously, we ultimately seek love as we do God. It is no wonder, therefore, that we refer to ourselves as "pilgrims" of love, placing it on a pedestal that is worthy of worship. This is, conceivably, a deeper reflection of Man's inherent longing to seek union with something much greater than himself – something that humbles him and alters his perception of 'truth', so he may transcend the parameters of the 'self' to discover the purpose and origins of his existence. As C.S. Lewis famously wrote, *"When we see the face of God, we shall know that we have always known it. He has moved moment by moment within all our earthly experiences of innocent love."*

    Bearing that in mind, it should not come as a surprise that the theme of love is commonly interspersed in almost all works of literature, presented as a reality independent of rules and predefined labels. It appears to build the very foundation of life, almost as if every other emotion is dependent on it – like the byproduct of an unpredictable chemical reaction. This is worth noting because in most cases, love is primarily associated with positivity. Anything that triggers a seemingly negative response is considered counterproductive and venomous, external to the process of "loving". This is a general misconception, whereby the lover denies the duality of love, unable to digest the paradoxical nature of this overwhelming truth. Since the world is created on the basis of duality, all opposing realities coexist to find meaning through each other. As such, love, too, finds meaning in its opposite, which is essentially pain, and uses it as a catalyst for spiritual, emotional and even physical evolution. However, since there are infinite shades of love, there are, likewise, infinite opposites that stand against it; it is up to the lover to accept the opposing reality as a reflection of his/her own inner darkness, and confront it peacefully. When we humbly surrender to the power of love, it begins to dictate our intentions and actions, eventually overcoming self-judgment, and instilling a kind of enlightened wisdom that only one, whose love is pure and truly unconditional in nature, is capable of experiencing. This concept has inevitably given birth to a variety of distinctive characters in literature and film, who have been immortalized as some of the most phenomenal lovers in history. Consequently, characters such as Romeo and Juliet, Triston and Isolde, Odysseus and Penelope – all seem to have set the standard of "unconditional love", allegorically symbolizing the intense passion, tragedy and insurmountable obstacles involved in any relationship that is based on it.

One of the major reasons why so much has been written extensively on love – and not just by novelists alone, but also by famous philosophers, astrologers, historians, mystics and even physicists – is the magnitude of mystery and 'magic' surrounding the euphoric nature of this phenomenon. Whether we discuss epic poetry or religious scriptures, love plays an important role in determining the course of events in the history of, both, fact and fiction. Many sacred texts, for instance, consider it to be one of the primary tenets of their respective faiths. In such cases, love is reflected through the life and teachings of iconic universal figures the likes of Jesus Christ, Buddha, Krishna, Mohammad – all of who are depicted as the physical embodiment of love in their own religion. This is when love is represented as an attribute of the Creator, drawing on the belief that whatever good exists within an individual is a reflection of God Himself. According to this philosophy, it is only through complete selflessness and obedient devotion to someone, that an individual inadvertently experiences a transformation which renews his/

her perspective of the world and sense of self. This transformation is different for everyone, often characterized by the individual's rejection of certain principles that were once held in high esteem. Typically, it is when lovers go against their normal disposition by doing that which is deemed unconventional for their nature. We can see the development of such changes in a range of literary characters, from William Shakespeare's famous *Hamlet*, whose "madness" is described as *"the very ecstasy of love/ Whose violent property fordoes itself... As oft as any passion under heaven....",* to the lethargic and smitten persona of Duke Orsino from *Twelfth Night*, who begins his monologue with the famous words, *"If music be the food of love, play on./ Give me excess of it that, surfeiting/ The appetite may sicken, and so die."* The prominent switch in behavior is, hence, a physical expression of one's internal battle between the logic of the mind and the impulse of the heart. In some cases, the change can be seen as the lover's metamorphosis from a selfish creature that was once consumed by the shadow of the Wasteland, to a compassionate and wise bearer of Light who sees beyond the limitations of the physical world. This is because after falling in love, the subject seeks to immortalize that feeling, longing for a life where the lover and beloved can be together for all eternity. The process of this transformation is crucial to the personal growth of an individual, marked by extreme highs and lows, whereby the lover is eventually bound to make a fundamental decision – whether the sacredness of love is worth all the suffering.

In this regard, love can easily be viewed as perhaps the most powerful of all catalysts, responsible for revolutionizing the very concept of self-discovery. This is explained elaborately through the Sufi doctrine of "divine love", made popular in the West by the influential writings of the 13th century Persian poet, Mevlana Jalal'uddin Rumi. The Sufis perceive life as a journey to explore love, attributing it to the evolutionary process of self-realization. Since love is believed to be a sacred Truth, the realization of this phenomenon is said to reveal the ultimate Reality of the universe, including one's own identity. This ideology is paralleled with the philosophical discussions of Socrates, which expound on the belief that, at one point, the individual is so consumed by the ecstasy of love, that he/she abandons what is perhaps his/her greatest possession – the "Self". This is a reference to the "Ego" which is the driving force behind all selfish desires. Before being exposed to true love, one is chained to and enslaved by the Ego, living in a self-constructed prison. The only way out of this prison is the individual's complete submission to love. After tasting the first few drops of love, a true lover surrenders completely to its sweet, intoxicating power, destroying the "Self" to pave way for a renewed identity through spiritual union. The Sufis refer to this concept as the annihilation of the Self to experience union with God, reiterating that the love felt for another human being is, in fact, a reflection of Man's love for the Creator. This is based on the fundamental belief that God dwells *"not in the skies or a throne, but within the hearts of the faithful"*; hence, to love another person is to love God Himself.

The philosophy of "divine love" is strongly intertwined with the notion of death, whence death of the Self is not the end; rather, it is a catalytic act of rebirth, creating a more evolved version of the individual, who is now stripped of all worldly and selfish impurities. It is often likened to the pressure that turns coal to a sparkling diamond, or the ashes that give rise to a phoenix in Eurasian mythology. This is perhaps one of the greatest reasons why we have obstacles, specifically separation, in almost every love story, wherein the element of separation poetically encapsulates the suffering and endurance of the lover(s). The nature of this separation may differ depending on the context of the relationship; however, in the test of true love, it always exists, leading to the origins of "forbidden love" which is considered to be one of the most self-gratifying genres of romance. In many cases, it is society that separates the lovers, as seen from the quintessential romance of *Romeo and Juliet*, and how their families keep them apart. Consequently, the star-crossed lovers choose to kill themselves rather than go through life without the beloved by their side. This is a perfect example of selfless love, where the purpose of life is defined by the object of one's affection, rather than by the lover him/herself. In this respect, we can perhaps interpret the phrase "falling in love" as the great fall of one's Ego, since the desire to unite with someone is placed higher than all other desires that exist. The longer two lovers are kept apart due to circumstances, the greater their agony. As an aftermath, their love continues to intensify until it transcends the parameters of time and space, ultimately reaching the metaphysical realm of Eternity.

The longing for "union" is most commonly interpreted as sexual desire. However, sex can also be seen as a very one-dimensional aspect of love, not necessarily a complete representation of the phenomenon, as suggested by famous philosophers as Plato, who gave birth to the concept of "platonic love". Theoretically, it is perceived as a physical manifestation of the spiritual union between two people who may or may not love each other, and as such, sex may or may not be conducive to the overall evolution of the individuals involved. It is only when the individuals are truly in love that the act of sex holds a special sacredness, owing to their mutual desire to dissolve in each other's essence and exist solely as "One". Sex based on love, therefore, underlines the merging of two souls that have been isolated from each other, celebrating their union after eons of separation (since the Spirit is considered an ancient entity). In retrospect, sex may even be interpreted as having little to do with the physical, and more to do with experiencing spiritual completion, as the Soul is said to be divided into dual counterparts before being sent into the physical plane, according to the law of Duality. Consequently, lovers travel through life searching for a missing piece of themselves; hence the reason why searching for love is reminiscent of searching for one's identity. In this respect, the carnal aspect of sex exists only because the Soul is confined within a temporary vehicle while placed in the realm of materialism – that vehicle is the human body. Thus, the expression of spiritual union becomes physical in nature; although it does not necessarily denote the Final union which may otherwise take place after the soul has transcended life on Earth and returned Home. Such interpretations help us understand the wholesome nature of 'romantic love' which disproves the widely held belief that it must exist solely between a husband and wife. It can, in fact, exist in absolutely any relationship, whence sex on the physical plane is only part of the attraction between two souls – not the essence of attraction itself. Therein, the range of love is potentially limitless, bearing the capacity to touch anyone or anything without discrimination – for instance, the love between a parent and child, two friends of the same or opposite sex, between animals, plants – or between any constituents of the cosmic order, where even something as scientific as the planets orbiting the Sun can be interpreted as an ecstatic expression of love. Here, the concept of "orbiting" is similar to the state of "whirling" – a meditative dance called *"Sama"* which gained popularity through Rumi when he was intoxicated by the musical vibrations of love felt for his spiritual master, Shams-i-Tabriz.

Through physical merging, the lovers come to experience a momentary glimpse of eternal union, sensed at the climax when the mind is believed to be entirely void of thought and memory, existing wholly in the present. It can, accordingly, be viewed as a unique, wordless expression of passionate love, which is presumably why so many artists speak of sex as a form of art. The passion present within the act of sex, however, may also be driven by lust rather than love, posing a significant question about the legitimacy of sexual desire. Here, the idea of "unconditional love" comes into play, as a true lover will always lay more emphasis on the happiness of the beloved than on one's own personal fulfillment – *"Your happiness is my happiness"*. This can be best observed in the stories of unrequited love, which are certainly more tragic than those centered on mutual love. This is because in the former, the lover not only has to bear the burden of obstacles on the path, but also digest the cold reality of rejection.

Throughout history, there have been people who have loved and lost, creating a whole new genre of romance based on isolation and despondency. As readers, we empathize with such characters, understanding the emotional and psychological implications of a broken heart. However, it is this very heartache that ultimately leads to the spiritual salvation of a lover, given that the love experienced is pure and unselfish in nature. This is symbolized in various literary pieces of work, including the famous Biblical accounts of Jesus who endured violent persecution at the hands of those very people to who he was sent as a savior. The whole idea of Jesus Christ having died for the sins of others, therefore, can be depicted as the epitome of true selflessness, drawing a fine line between those who love in order to be loved, and those who choose to love for the greater good. This is why the Christian doctrine emphasizes on the need to *"love thy enemy"*, because the love we feel for those who care for us is conditional and transient – hence, unable to reach the scope of eternity. To love someone who has wronged us is a test that most of us are unable to pass simply because it requires the destruction of human expectation, so that one may love simply for the sake of loving. Contextually, loving a person despite being rejected is not a sign of weakness, and can alternately be seen as a mark of enlightenment, for the individual recognizes that it is not the person who is worthy of resentment, rather the act of rejection itself that is the root of pain. Since the lover is not concerned with reciprocation, the love remains unconditional as long as it is nourished and sustained by the lover. Otherwise, it can very easily die just as any other form of life when not taken care of. This is why there are often parallels drawn between love and nature – both alive with the remembrance of someone special.

    As with all drugs, love yields different reactions from everyone – some embrace it with open arms, while others go in denial. The poignancy of elation, however, that is frequently attributed to love takes shape in the form of wild, ecstatic bliss, causing the lover to do things that would seem unusual or even questionable to the rest of the world. In the words of Plato, *"At the touch of love, everyone becomes a poet"*. The lover may even appear to be on the brink of insanity, when, conversely, it may also be the first time that he/she is able to view things with absolute clarity. If the lover is convinced that what is felt is real, there is no force in the world that can change his/her perception of reality because it is founded on something much greater than mere words or ideals – it is founded on the strength of belief. This leads to a subtle interplay between reality and illusion, where the real and the apparent are not necessarily the same, and "reality" is entirely subject to interpretation and experience. Paradoxically, it is often said that rather than blurring reality, love seeks to reveal that which cannot be deciphered or grasped entirely by those who have never been exposed to the feeling of absolute submission. This is why the concept of love is commonly expressed through magic-infused descriptions, taking us into a strange world where the hybridized face of reality appears to be nothing less than a bizarre, magical dream. The surrealism associated with the sensation of love is, therefore, almost pivotal in portraying the degree of intensity and exhilaration involved, where the elements of 'fantasy' become necessary in capturing the emotion with all its colors and complexities.

The clarity of belief that is strongly tied to love is defined by an inscrutable sense of power and mystery, which is presumably why so many of the greatest leaders in history have spoken of it as an omnipotent force of Creation, similar to the force of God. Indeed, various examples from the past illustrate the overwhelming power of love as a source of change all over the world. In the West, individuals such as Martin Luther King laid great emphasis on humanity's potential to love everyone and everything as if it were the singular purpose of existence – a belief that not only helped to salvage the rights and freedom of the African American community, but simultaneously revived the hope of living in an equal and just society. Similar examples exist in the East, such as Mahatma Gandhi, whose adherence to non-violence and love can be traced back to the ancient philosophy of Gautama Buddha, who received Enlightenment by realizing that the answer to all suffering is complete selflessness. In this regard, love is perhaps the only form of life that is invulnerable to the corruption of power and politics, with the ability to light up the darkest of places. This is why it is not restricted to specific parts of the world, because its vast dimension has the capacity to be a universal phenomenon rather than an idea that caters strictly to a particular place, situation or race of people. We can see this from the way love has been addressed time and time again in the political speeches of famous presidents, the songs and music of extraordinary artists, and the beautifully poignant verses of inspirational poets – all at the peak of their success and fame, most of who even ended up sacrificing their lives to ensure their voices were heard.

Politicians the likes of Abraham Lincoln and John F. Kennedy are excellent cases in point who stressed highly on using love as a tool to bring a positive revolution, with the latter clearly stating in a famous political sermon, *"If you make peaceful revolution impossible, you make violent revolution inevitable."* It suddenly becomes increasingly obvious why such leaders were assassinated – being the only handful who focused on humanity's need to collectively evolve, rather than pursuing personal greed for greater control. Such incidents portray love as a divine culmination of all forms of life whose astounding power, if exposed to the common man, could potentially threaten the foundations of tyranny and oppression. Popular musicians too have, since long, incorporated love into the lyrics and compositions of their music – some, such as the Beatles, using it to promote the peaceful "Hippie movement" that revolutionized the 60's. John Lennon ultimately became an emblem of universal love, addressing it in almost all his interviews and music, *"If someone thinks that love and peace is a cliché that must have been left behind in the Sixties, that's his problem. Love and peace are eternal".* A classic example relevant here is the widely-celebrated reggae music of Bob Marley, almost all of which speaks of love as a force for liberation and independence, standing against political fascism. Similarly, Jimi Hendrix, one of the greatest electric guitarists in music history, made statements that aligned with Lennon and Marley's philosophy of love as a catalyst for socio-political change, *"When the power of love overcomes the love of power, the world will know peace".* Interestingly, Lennon and Marley were both assassinated, similar to the aforementioned presidents, and Hendrix's untimely death is, to this day, subject to great controversy as people still speculate about the likelihood of a conspiracy.

Such examples are also prevalent in the history of Eastern musicians and poets – the more prominent ones having left behind a legacy that has greatly impacted Eastern and Western audiences alike. This can be exemplified through the unparalleled talent of famous Qawwali singer, Nusrat Fateh Ali Khan, whose exceptional talent in the arena of Sufi folk music (that glorifies divine love) influenced the lyrics and compositions of renowned Western musicians such as Jeff Buckley, Eddie Vedder from *Pearl Jam* and Peter Gabriel, along with legendary Eastern musicians the likes of A. R. Rahman and Azerbaijani singer, Alim Qasimov. Khan's unconventional music, similar to the marvelous poetry of Rumi, Khalil Gibran, Farid'uddin Attar and Omer Khayyam, came to be seen as exuberant utterances of love, hence the reason it continues to attract people from different corners of the world, proving that love, like music, knows no borders. It serves as a beautiful reminder of how the power of love, applied anywhere, can eradicate prejudice, and unite the world on the basis of mutual respect and tolerance.

Today, the world seems to have been greatly cut off from what was once deemed necessary for the revival of the human spirit. Much of this has to do with our detachment from nature, whose nurturing, maternal qualities have paid homage to the celestial power of love since time immemorial. Without recognizing the connection between nature and love, societies will continue to stagnate, investing their energies into a machine that serves the purpose of only those in control. Regardless of one's belief or disbelief regarding the existence of a Supreme deity, we can unanimously agree that the infinite bounties of nature selflessly provide for the livelihood of all, including those who neglect or exploit it. Such unconditional servitude is perhaps the greatest and most admirable expression of love, whose purpose of existence is defined exclusively by the will to serve and appease. This is one of the elementary truths of the Universe, elaborated through the Dharma of Buddhist texts in the words, *"Love is beauty and beauty is truth; and that is why in the beauty of a flower, we can see the truth of the universe".* It is no wonder, therefore, that most of the major religions of the world make countless references to the sanctity of nature, some minor ones even equating it to the embodiment of God Himself, such as the Native American tribes of North America. This is where the belief in paganism takes its course, whereby the spirit of the gods is believed to be associated with the different components of nature.

With all its power, the concept of universal love can perhaps easily serve as a solution to all fundamental problems of the world. This ideology is favored by a contemporary spiritual movement that is popularly referred to as "The Green Revolution USA". The movement, founded by Azhar Shah Faridie, developed as a result of a simple observation made by Shah - that the misery of life stems not from adapting to the new world, but from dismissing the sacredness of the old world, which is equally, if not more, crucial to the evolution of human consciousness. By embracing one and denouncing the other, the essence of love is lost due to a blatant imbalance within the cosmic order. The movement, consequently, encourages the plantation of trees, plants and flowers in the name of wise spiritual leaders, saints or prominent figures who sought to change the world in the name of Love – figures such as Jesus Christ, Krishna, Buddha, Abdul Baha, Mohammad, Guru Nanak, etc. This is so people of different faiths and backgrounds, with all their perfections and imperfections, can come forth to create global harmony. Believing nature to be alive with the remembrance of God, Shah attributes it to the ultimate source of love which, if not realized, will only lead to the degeneration of humanity. By paying respect to nature, and simultaneously reviving the names of those who preached the sacred doctrine of Love, the movement introduces peace and tolerance as a gateway to global prosperity. Many consider this is to be a fascinating example of how the catalytic properties of love can literally and figuratively change the course of life as we know it.

After delving into the diverse connotations that are attached to love, one may find it easier to assess why many of the greatest works of literature make solid correlations between the prophecy of the coming Age and the radical strength of love as a force for social and physical transformation in the world. This enables us to understand the significant theme of "good versus evil" in terms of those who will either stand for the power of love, or against it. Many ancient scriptures, particularly belonging to monotheistic religions, for instance, discuss the Last Age as an era wherein love will be instrumental in saving the righteous from the overwhelming satanic influence of deception and wrongdoing, *"At that time... because of the increase of wickedness, the love of most will grow cold" (Matthew, 24:10-12).* We can observe this specifically in sacred texts from Christianity, Judaism and Islam, in which the Final Stage of earthly life is defined by the emergence of a holy envoy who will advocate love as a way to bring peace and prosperity into the world. Christians refer to this emergence as the resurrection of Jesus – a prophecy that is shared with Muslims, whereby he is believed to revive the spirit of compassion and glory that has been lost since his early days on Earth. Additionally, the Muslim faith sheds light on a precursor to the emergence of Jesus, evasively referred to as the "Mahdi" (*The Guided One)*, who is believed to sow the seeds of love in preparation for the grand arrival of Jesus, and his confrontation with the Antichrist. This is an interesting addition to detail that many literary scholars interpret as a well-kept secret, whereby many Muslims reject the concept of the Mahdi out of sheer disillusionment which stems from the hopelessness of the modern age. Several renowned authors, however, have taken inspiration from this depiction of the Last Age, incorporating it into many of their writings. One of these is J. R. R. Tolkien's famous *The Lord of the Rings* trilogy. The story can be seen as a stunning allegorical portrayal of the Final Hour, whence the Fellowship of Nine overcomes all odds to save Middle Earth from the malice of the Dark Lord, *Sauron.* As the story develops, we see that it is only through love and selfless conviction, showcased in varying shades through different relationships, that the fellowship, with the help of nature, restores the rule of Man once again on Middle Earth – highly reminiscent of the restoration of Christ at the End of Times.

This concept, however, is not limited to monotheistic religions alone, and can also be found in several other scriptures, including Hindu literature – perhaps the only difference being the slight divergence of certain names. The dawning of a new Era, which is also attributed to the Aztec and Mayan civilizations, is said to awaken the female energy of the universe, leading to a Higher Consciousness that is crafted by the revolution of love. This new era, referred to by astrologers as *"The Age of Aquarius"* is believed to be the year 2012, wherein the violent and destructive energy of the "Masculine" is said to be overpowered by the gentle and protective energy of the "Divine Feminine". Hindus consider this to be the age in which the last and final incarnation of Vishnu, known as *Kalki* (Destroyer of Ignorance), will bring an end to the injustices of the world by upholding the principles of truth and love in a spiritually stagnant society, *"For the protection of the good and for the destruction of evil, and for the establishment of righteousness, I come into being age after age. (Gita: 4.7–8)"*. Similarly, Buddhists consider this spiritual leader to be the final incarnation of Siddharta Gautama Buddha, whose love is believed to guide the world out of darkness and despair. In this case, what is worth noting is the distinct similarities present within the scriptures – with almost all of them highlighting the emergence of a man who will change the course of human history, not through weapons or technology, nor arrogance or power, but through the sole demonstration of love as a force that breathes life into the world, starting all things anew.

Such grand illustrations of love allow us to elevate the position of this phenomenon to new heights where it no longer exists merely as a means to fill the void, and instead challenges the socially constructed horizons of perception and life. The more one tries to hold on to the feeling, the more it struggles to escape – this is why one of the most self-defining aspects of love is freedom, for being possessive is a feeling that is strictly opposed to the essence of love. By taking the first plunge into the ocean of love, one welcomes the thrill of complete liberation, hence the reason why a number of movements use it as a tool to break free from the shackles of slavery, exploitation, ownership, oppression and injustice. If ever fallen "out of love", it is only a matter of time before one, inevitably, reflects on the road not taken. This is considered to be one of the most painful experiences in life, as the pangs of regret are described by many to be a lot worse than the feeling of rejection. Understandably, the consequences of ignoring someone's love is regarded by many, particularly the Sufis, to be a heinous crime – one that takes a lifetime to pay off, and even then it is up to the lover to forgive the person in question. If the purpose of life is defined by an exploration of love, and it is, henceforth, placed on a pedestal above all else in the world, it becomes clear as to why toying with someone's feelings or deliberately rejecting his/her love may constitute as an act against God, for it reveals one's inability to recognize that which is truly sacred and divine.

Perhaps if we think less about understanding love and instead focus more on experiencing it in a given moment – no matter how brief or ephemeral – we may come one step closer in our attempt to truly evolve. When finally experienced, love further intensifies in sensation, revealing the expansive dimensions of its being, and diminishing the boundaries of what was once believed to be "the real and the absolute". This is a journey to the Infinite, to Nothingness, where the paradox of love is unraveled as the greatest, most maddening Truth, imperative for the process of awakening. Entering the realm of love is, hence, fittingly analogous to the act of renewal, whence to be "something", the lover must dissolve into "nothing". What we ultimately learn is that the self-seeking curiosity which begins our journey – "Does love exist?" – is organically morphed into a profound exploration of "Do I exist?"

–One who loves

I Don't Know Why

I don't know why I love you
I don't know why I cry
I don't know why I try
because you just keep pushing me away

I don't know why I care
Why do I even bother?
Because you don't love me back
I don't know why I try to hide my feelings
because they always come back out
I don't know why I keep telling myself
It's going to be all right
when it's not

I don't know why I keep clinging to you
I don't know why I'm so attracted to you
I don't know why these feelings came
or why they won't go away

I don't know why I need you
I don't know why I go crazy
Just thinking of you
I don't know why I can't live without you
I don't know why I hate you so much
but I love you just the same
I don't even know why
I feel this way

Just Because

Just because I love you
Doesn't mean
I don't hate you
Just because you're my world
doesn't mean
I have to revolve around you
Just because I care about you
Doesn't mean
I will help you up when you fall
Just because I love your voice
Doesn't mean
I won't tune you out when you talk
Just because I believe the things you tell me
Doesn't mean
I'm going to let them get to me
And just because I love you
Doesn't mean
That I don't hate you

Why?

Why do I love you?
Stop making me love you
Why do I love your smile?
Stop smiling at me
You know I love it when you do
So why do you keep doing it?
Why do I love your voice?
Stop talking around me
You know I love it when you do
So why do you keep doing it?
Why do I love your eyes?
Stop looking at me
You know I love it when you do
So why do you keep doing it?
Why do I love you?
Stop being near me
You know I'm just going to love you more
So why do you keep doing it?
Why do I love you?
Stop making me love you

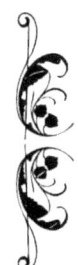

Missing You Not (Part III)

When I sit here
and think of you
I try not to remember all the things
we went through
while I was there
where were you?
I'll give you one thing that's true
I realized
it wasn't you I missed
it was me

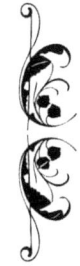

Me and You

I walk over to you
you put your hand in mine
I look into your eyes
your warm arms holding me
my head on your shoulder
your good sent clogging up my nose
I could care less if we stay
there for hours
you gaze into my eyes
I lean forward
your eyes closing
as my lips meet yours
we pull away
I hear you mutter those words
I wanted to hear for a long time
I love you
that's when I wake up
from my dream
smiling
until the next one comes
with me and you

You're It (Me and You – Part II)

You're there, I'm here
You talk, I smile
You blink, I look away
You smile, I stop
Breathing, until I realize
you looked away too.
You lean forward, I'm
smiling
my heart is racing.
You look away while I do the
same
you love me but I can't
you're looking at me, I can't
and look around instead

Time slows as I look at you
We're not moving and I'm
not thinking
then there's a rush
time gets faster and you're mine

I'm here, you're there
I smile, you talk
I look away, you blink
I stop breathing, you smile
and look away too
I want to say something, you
stop me
I forgot but I still know

Time seems to be slower
again, till it stops
completely.
I search for words
I feel what you feel
You see what I see
you read my mind
I have your hand
Time flies away
You turn and it's over
I smile then stop

I'm here and you're not.
It wasn't real but I liked it
I blink and breathe again
and go back to sleep.

Denial (Part I)

I hate that I love you
But even though it's true
It hurts even thinking of you
Even when you're passing me by
I don't look and try
Not to think of all the lies
You told me
And all I do is smile
Because as you're living your life
I'm living mine
Loving to hate you
Even though it's not true

Denial Part 2

I hate you
But I love you
I hate the way you make me feel
but I love you
I hate to love you
but I still love you
I hate to look at you
but I'm still looking
I hate to be near you
but I'm still walking toward you
I hate to think of you
but you're still on my mind
I hate you
I hate you
I hate you
but I love you.

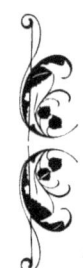

No Point

There was this guy
when I looked in his eyes
I would see all the stars in the sky
they glistened as he spoke
he was the world
the one who controlled
my emotions
my dreams

How could one person control so much
but knew little about it?
When I heard him speak
his words would stay in the
air all around me
as I inhale them slowly into my body
he was the only one there in my eyes
in a room crowded with people
I sometimes wondered if he were mine
Would I shine like the sun
in his eyes?
Would I occupy his dreams
like he does mine?
I could never stop the questions
was I the one he saw when he
closed his eyes?
Was I the person whose voice
he enjoyed hearing?
What if the dreams I had
for so long came true

There was this guy
he spent most of his time
in my head, in my heart
in my dreams
I finally realized that was never
going to change
how was it possible
to get the world off your shoulders?
Off your mind?
And get left with nothing
this was something no one could change
there was no point
and I gave up on it.

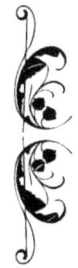

Some thoughts

What am I thinking?
Is it you I fear?
Or is it something I'm afraid to hear

I look at you
looking at me
wondering if you're thinking the same

Hurting

Every time I look at you
I'm wishing you were mine
every time I think of you
I'm wishing you were with me
Every time I smile at you
I'm wishing you think of me too

Every time you're with me
I'm wishing that I could look
at you and not
feel the way I feel
every time you smile at me
I'm wishing I could turn my
eyes somewhere else
every time you look at me
I'm wishing that my heart
would stop skipping beats

Every time I close my eyes
I'm wishing that you weren't there
sometimes I wish that you love me
as much as I love you
most of the time I wish that
I don't love you at all

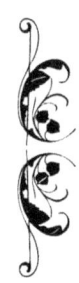

No Luck

Every day is painful without you
every day is useless without you
every day I wish you were there
every day I wish you could stay

Everything else is wonderful
when I'm with you
everything else doesn't
matter when I'm with you
everything I wish is about you
everything I wish is for you

No one is like you
there is no one I care for as
much as you
I'm wishing for you
I'm wishing for me

I have no luck
because I wish every day
for the same thing
and nothing happens

I'm Confused

I hate when I'm with you
I hate when I'm without you
Why can I make up my mind?
I hate thinking about you
I can't stop thinking about you
Why can I make up my mind?

I love not thinking of you
so I won't have to remember
Your eyes, Your smile, Your face, You
Is my mind made up?

I hate not thinking of you
then I won't remember
Your eyes, Your smile, Your face, You
Why can't I make up my mind?

Is my mind made up?
Why can't I make up my mind
I love you, I need you
I hate you, I want you

I can never make up my mind

Those Moments

at times I wish I never met you
at times I wish I was still in your heart
like you are mine
at times I feel mad
at times I feel sad
but in reality I know
we were never meant to be.
How come my heart can't see that?

My eyes are wondering
my heart is searching
my soul is hoping
and everything always leads back to you

Circles

The more I think of you
the more I want to stop
but every time I do think of you
the more I like you
the only reason I started is
because you stopped.

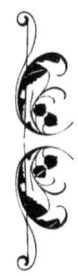

Icon

My stomach hurts
my heart stopped
my shoulders are heavy
my mind is racing
I can't think straight
I can't breathe
I... I think I love you

Stupid Little Love Song

Why do I keep allowing myself
to cry over you?
You're never here to catch all
the tears?
What I fear most is
what will happen when
you realize all those
tears are for you.
But then again even
if you knew
I'd still be crying
but for the reason of
you know how I feel and
you will never care

What is Love?

Love is like a dream
it feels real but its distant
it's invisible but you're
caught up in it.

Love is like a dream
when you wake up from that dream
it all falls apart; everything changes

When you try to close your eyes again
the dream is different
you can't get it to the
original one where
everything feels right.

Ask me if I ever been in love
I'll say only in my dreams
that's why I never have them

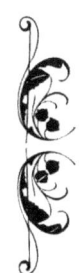

Words Form

More and more I wonder
what you mean to me
the more I wonder the more
closer I get to
you and the words form in
my head to say
I love you

Without Feeling

I feel like I should be doing
something
I just don't know what
I feel like I want something
like I need something
I feel like I should be
somewhere
but I'm not
I'm standing here spinning
waiting to stop
waiting to feel myself go
to what I want

I feel like I should be with
you
where are you?
I feel like I should be
breathing
like I should show how I feel
but I'm not
I'm standing here alone
waiting to feel like I belong
waiting to understand
waiting to feel myself do
what I want to
but without feeling

Broken

Spinning
like my head
round you go
cracking
my neck
breaking
my way through stone
leaning
my body on the clouds
slowly
I will show
how fast I would not fall,
you're
touching
my hand
wishing
you won't, come to
know
how I feel
scratching
while you watch me
shut
you
out.

Hating This

Every time I see you
I get a little weak
but then I think to myself
why can't I do better

I always try to hide
away from what I keep inside
how can this be
when you don't even notice me?
When I close my eyes
I don't want you there
when I look over to see you
you look over to see her ...

I hate that I love you because you will
never know

Notice Me

Hello?
Why do I have to scream at the
top of my lungs for you
to hear me?
It still doesn't help,
you blink and look away.
I want you to see me,
but I forgot you were blind.
I want you to hear me,
but I forgot you were deaf.
I try and I try but
it always fails.
Then when I see you
fall to the ground
I feel small because
even if I do help you
up
you will see no one there.

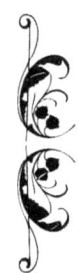

Music is Love

My life is a whole bunch of
music lyrics.
It's not like I'm trying to avoid
them.
I just can't seem to write
my own story
I have so much to say
but is that too much?
Because I can never get the
words out.

Change

My mind is always racing.
There are some things I still think about.
Some things never change.
One thing I've noticed is
when I slow down and
let my thoughts breathe
it's you I'm thinking about.
The feelings you give me are
something I can't describe.
But why should I have to?
I'm with you now and
everything is different.

My New Life

here I am trying to
write again
alone with my pen
and my paper
the only thing that seemed to listen.
I feel like I turned my
back on something that was real,
that was safe.
Is it wrong that I want that
feeling again?
but you can't turn your back on
something and expect it to be
the same.
I let my pen down, and
myself.
I was looking in all the wrong
places
to find me
to find the trust, the confidence
what I didn't realize
was, that boxed <u>myself</u>
away along with
other emotions I was
trying to hide from.
the truth hurts they say
I couldn't handle it
before
but I'm strong enough now
to face what I've buried.
I say it's different now
because before I was truly
alone
now I have you.

No Explanation

Suppress
Emotions
Release
Thoughts

Listen

That's what you hear
anyways.
You can't choose to
listen halfway through
the story.
My story.
And even when I tried
to get some answers
I realized there was
no question.
No one listened
so I did.
Words piled high
with nowhere to
spill.
Powerful words
leads to controlling
thoughts.
Words are supposed
to hurt.
But I realized that
wasn't the case.
I realized too late
that I needed to
listen to me
I was worried about

being heard, I
forgot to listen to myself
when I did listen
I heard, "this is
just the beginning."
Realizing "too late"
was the best thing
that ever happened to me.
So I don't need you to
listen anymore.
I don't care if I'm
Heard
At the end of the day
I'm still going to be
Myself
and I tell myself no one
can stop you from
being you.
Now that is worth
listening to!

Untitled

I'm always thinking
always dreaming
I'm blind 'cus
I don't see from the
inside out,
rather outside in. There is a difference
what's right, what to do?
What's a dream though?
Silly thoughts that take you
where you want to go.
I want to move on but
it seems like something is
holding me back. I'm comfortable
but is this the only thing?
I like to talk, but maybe
I should just listen.
This is what happens when
I don't listen to myself.
A day can't change your feelings
and feelings can't change in a day.
TRUST
is a strong word.
Maybe it's me,
maybe I don't trust myself
I need something different
to get away.

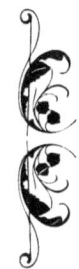

Pain Hurdles

I'm reading my life again
painful memories
trapped inside words.
What can I do?
What should I say?
I know I have a lot
but something is missing.
When there is a hole
in your heart, it can
only be filled in a certain way.
It's like coming to a dead end
on a one-way street.
Why am I complaining?
Is there something wrong?
Pain doesn't last forever
but it's the hardest to get
over.

Relapse

Why do I feel so alone?
What is it that I want?
My mind keeps going
back to you.
But I feel like I'm losing you.
My heart is filling me
with pain songs
and my eyes are letting the
sounds flow.
But who is going to hear me?
Why do I feel like I'm back
where I started?
Naïve I am.
Filling my head with
the fantasies, lies, dreams.
Stupid, selfish me.
Not worrying about others' needs
just mine.
But then I asked myself
what <u>do</u> I really need?
I want you is that the
problem? Or do I just want
myself to be happy
that I'm losing my sight…
Are they right? Should I listen?
I don't know but all I know is
there's no one to ask because
there's no one here
I'm alone. Again.

Open-ended Questions

I need someone to hold me.
I thought it be you
but your arms weren't
there.
They never came.
Maybe if you would've
took the time to share
your warmth, then I
wouldn't feel like this
now.
Acid filled tears, burn
flesh as they slowly
roll down my face.
What am I doing all this for?
Simple questions too complex
to answer
even for myself.
Overthinking or under asking.
I don't know what they
have been directed to.

Wrong Channel

The look in your eyes are different.
Different than they were yesterday.
I can feel it, something is
missing.
I can sense it, something is
wrong.
The picture's off.

Distance

Why haven't I heard from you?
I'm starting to worry if
you ever wonder about me.
I'm starting to worry about you.
Where are you?
What are you doing?

Do you care how I'm feeling?
I'm starting to feel like
I'm not important to you.
You are important to me.
Do you care?
Do you think about me?

Do you love me?
You told me you did
but is it real?
I love you
Am I important?
Do you notice?

Why haven't I heard from you today?
I don't feel a connection
the distance is growing.
Where are you?
Do you care?
Am I important?

Breakthrough

This life is so stressful
only if you make it so.
I can feel my soul searching
my mind wandering
my heart yearning
for the answer to the questions
I have yet to find.
I feel like I'm stuck in
neutral with no one to give
me the push I need to go
where I want to go.
Where that is I do not
know.

So maybe it's me.
Maybe I'm limiting myself
by thinking too much
about where I am going
rather than where I am.
Now I am going to let my soul rest
slow my mind down
let my heart do its job.
No more stressing about what's
to come.
I'm going to live life to
the fullest.
Now.

Light at the End

Everything I look for,
everything I lack
I see in you.
I didn't know I was
waiting for you
but I realized I was
crying out for you.
Angel with no wings
saved me from myself.
You changed my
life, because
when I'm with you
everything is brighter.
You have
comfort, security,
tenderness,
this is something new,
but I like it.
Everything is clearer
now, this is
where I'm supposed to be.

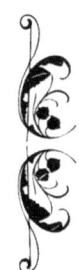

His Lips

Ooh I kiss your lips
I kiss your lips
and I melt.
I close my eyes
and I kiss your lips
and I melt
melt into you
melt into something I never
thought I'd be
I want to stay here
forever.
Pressed against your lips.
Soft, sexy, strong
and safe.
I kiss your lips
and I am safe.
I kiss your lips
and I know this is exactly
where I'm supposed to be

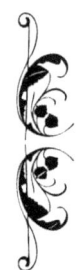

I Found You

It's not like I was searching for you
but I was wishing
hoping someone would come along
and save me from myself.

Someone to be strong for me
someone to understand me
someone to always be there for me

So I waited for you.
I knew if I was patient
I would find the person I was
meant to be with.

When I found you
I knew it was you that
I dreamed about.
And I was ready for you.

Finally! I said to myself
I can start living
because with you I am alive
I am happy.

All the wishing turned out
to come true.
I found you and
I'm never letting go.

I am in love.

*"Between me and You, there is only me.
Take away the me so only You remain."*
—Mansur Al Hallaj

Use these pages to document your journey of love.

ABOUT THE AUTHOR

S. D. Webb is an American creative writer and poet. She is a senior majoring in Entrepreneurship at Suffolk University in Boston, Massachusetts. She enjoys writing as an act of expression and she loves music and cooking.

Join the conversation on Facebook
https://www.facebook.com/loveis.sdwebb

Twitter: InnovaPub

Website: www.innovative-publishers.com

Email: pub@innovative-publishers.com

Blog: http://innovativepublishers.blogspot.com/

http://www.facebook.com/InnovativePublishers

www.ingramcontent.com/pod-product-compliance
Lightning Source LLC
LaVergne TN
LVHW051839080426
835512LV00018B/2975